Matthew Finkle and Brittain Sullivan

CHRONICLE BOOKS

SAN FRANCISCO

Library of Congress Cataloging-in-Publication Data

Finkle, Matthew.

 I love my bike / Matthew Finkle and Brittain Sullivan.
   p. cm.
 ISBN 978-1-4521-0048-7
1. Cycling. 2. Cycling—United States—Pictorial works. 3. Cyclists—United States—Pictorial works. I. Sullivan, Brittain. II. Title.
 GV1041.F56 2011
 796.6—dc22

                    2010030919

Manufactured in China

Designed by Chris Piascik

10 9 8 7 6 5 4 3 2 1

Chronicle Books LLC
680 Second Street
San Francisco, CA 94107
www.chroniclebooks.com

HIEU NGUYEN

AGE: 35 / HOMETOWN: TEMECULA, CA

Matt and I love everything about bicycles. It is no small coincidence that we met on a bike ride with mutual friends one of the few clear summer nights in Boston during a month when it poured down rain twenty-two of thirty days. From that night on, our sense of adventure took us anywhere we could imagine on our bikes. We would wake up very early every morning before work to meet up with a group of friends and ride to get coffee and breakfast somewhere we had never been, and punctuated our days with late-night rides to Castle Island or Walden Pond or through the desolate streets of downtown Boston in the wee hours of the morning. It was one of the most memorable summers of our lives, filled end to end with journeys through beautiful landscapes and with good company.

We didn't want it to end, but the days started to get shorter, the temperature became cooler, and our familiar bike routes began to look a little less green. For Matt and me, our shared excitement for all things cycling was only surpassed by the great friends that we met along the way. It was then that we thought to combine our skills and love of bicycles, and we set out to travel the country photographing people and their bikes.

This book is not about a singular style of bike or type of cycling but rather about all of us in a grand kinship of bicycles. We wanted to capture the strength, willpower, and grit, as well as the creativity, sense of humor, and whimsy of riding a bike.

Matt and I began photographing our cycling friends around Boston and taking short treks to New Hampshire, New York City, and Philadelphia to track down people riding their bikes. We met so many great people on these first trips. Almost everyone we stopped and asked to pose with his or her bicycle answered, "I love my bike!"—our sentiment exactly!

Throughout our travels—eventually we made it all the way west to Pacific Coast cities from Portland to Los Angeles—Matt and I have had the tremendous pleasure of being in the company of many people of great importance to their respective cycling cultures, but they stand side by side with a community of people who are, quite simply, cyclists like us. In each city and town that we visited, people shared with us their earliest recollections of learning to ride a bike, and we were led through all of the windy streets and back roads or alleys, over terrain familiar only to a cyclist who spends many days committing them to muscle-memory. The journey was greater than anything we could have imagined: we had so much fun meeting cyclists of all ages and backgrounds, geeking-out on bike components, and also taking in a few solitary moments with the landscape of the places we found ourselves.

Matt and I set out to find fellow enthusiasts of humankind's greatest invention. What we found were friends whom we hope to know for a lifetime . . . along with their bicycles.

—Brittain Sullivan

David Krebs &
Bob Driscoll

HOMETOWN: GLOUCESTER, MA

BRENTON SALO

AGE: 29 / HOMETOWN: PORTLAND, OR

THE Chain IS THE HEART of the DRIVETRAIN!

Gregg Minasian

HOMETOWN: ST. LOUIS, MI
CURRENT CITY: BOSTON, MA

Gregg is fond of discussing at length the merits of a good chain and its importance as a component on your bicycle. "The chain is the heart of the drivetrain!" It's either that, or "Where's your helmet?!"

I have spent my entire
Life trying to re-create
the way that I felt as
a child when the training
wheels were first taken
off of my bicycle.

TAYLOR YODER

AGE: 19 / HOMETOWN: WASHINGTON, D.C.
CURRENT CITY: NEW YORK, NY

CARSON CRAM

HOMETOWN: SAVANNAH, GA
CURRENT CITY: PHILADELPHIA, PA

MICAH "BUBBA" HOLBROOK

AGE: 23 / HOMETOWN: ORLANDO, FL
CURRENT CITY: SEATTLE, WA

ERIC STRATTON

AGE: 29
HOMETOWN: TALLAHASSEE, FL
CURRENT CITY: BOSTON, MA

MIKE SHOWED US HOW TO SPOT THE OUT-OF-TOWNERS BY WATCHING THEM STRUGGLE UP THE STEEPEST HILLS IN AN EGO-FUELED DEATH MARCH.

Mike "Giant" LeSage

AGE: 39 / HOMETOWN: ALBUQUERQUE, NM CURRENT CITY: SAN FRANCISCO, CA

Mike loves thrashing down the busy streets of San Francisco. Cycling is his knife and is reflected in many of his drawings—and in the Major Taylor tattoo on the back of his right hand. During our visit to his studio, Mike showed us how to spot the out-of-towners by watching them struggle up the steepest hills in an ego-fueled death march. San Francisco natives, having less to prove, will detour a block or two over to ride the more mellow climb.

24

IAN SUTTON

AGE: 26 / FRAME BUILDER, ICARUS CYCLES
HOMETOWN: BOULDER, CO
CURRENT CITY: BOSTON, MA

Come back around midnight.
BMX riders take over this park!

Brennan Jakiroa

AGE: 26 / HOME COUNTRY: NEW ZEALAND
CURRENT CITY: NEW YORK, NY

RANDON
MARTIN

AGE: 19 / HOMETOWN: CLEARWATER, FL
CURRENT CITY: PHILADELPHIA, PA

"I remember racing my brother around the
cul-de-sac in our neighborhood when we
were 8 or 9 years old. That is when we first
discovered the fun and pain of jousting
each other's spokes with sticks."

I SERENADE THE STREETS!

Sierra Carrere

AGE: 23
HOMETOWN: ITHACA, NY
CURRENT CITY: NEW YORK, NY

MATT LINGO

800

MATT CARDINAL

AGE: 37 / FRAME BUILDER, SIGNAL CYCLES
HOMETOWN: SLAVE LAKE, AB, CANADA
CURRENT CITY: PORTLAND, OR

Rosalind Patterson

AGE: **20** / HOMETOWN: RADNOR, PA
CURRENT CITY: BOSTON, MA

glenn
Hays

HERNAN MONTENEGRO

AGE: **23**
HOMETOWN: SANTA MONICA, CA

Jaiko Suzuki

HOMETOWN: TOKYO, JAPAN
CURRENT CITY: NEW YORK, NY

"You have to ride your bike through Times Square at night! Cycling through the streets of the city is like being in *Batman* or *Spider-Man*—buildings fly above your head as you ride on."

MATTHEW SIPPLE

AGE: **26**
HOMETOWN: FORT MITCHELL, KY
CURRENT CITY: SEATTLE, WA

ALEX SULLIVAN

AGE: 24 / HOMETOWN: BOSTON, MA

"I am always looking for the next hairpin, breathtaking ride. Sometimes I just start riding in a city or state I've never been to, and I let GPS find my way home. Sometimes you have to get lost to find the best ride."

MONSTER
CONCESSIONS

JOE
BOUDREAU

AGE: 27
HOMETOWN: SALEM, NH
CURRENT CITY: BOSTON, MA

"I'll take my bike over a girl any day.
This Geekhouse? Best ride ever."

STEVE SCHINNERER

AGE: 24
HOMETOWN: MARBLEHEAD, MA
CURRENT CITY: BOSTON, MA

justin keena

AGE: **26**
HOMETOWN: WESTMINSTER, MA
CURRENT CITY: BOSTON, MA

CAITLIN MENOTTI

AGE: 24
HOMETOWN: GENEVA, NY
CURRENT CITY: BOSTON, MA

KEITH TEKET

AGE: 27
HOMETOWN: BALTIMORE, MD

ALEX FARIOLETTI

AGE: 31
HOMETOWN: SAN FRANCISCO, CA

aaron panone

AGE: **26**
HOMETOWN: TWIN CITIES, MN
CURRENT CITY: BOSTON, MA

I'VE BEEN KNOWN TO DROOL OVER DROPOUTS!

JOHN "PROLLY" WATSON

HOMETOWN: WILMINGTON, NC
CURRENT CITY: BROOKLYN, NY

Prolly can often be found hucking himself off a set of stairs, going big at the Brooklyn Banks, or charging through the streets of New York City ... or, of course, holding court in one of the most-followed cycling-culture blogs worldwide.

CHRISTOPHER FONSECA

AGE: **26** / HOMETOWN: SAN FRANCISCO, CA

ReID Offringa

AGE: 26
HOMETOWN: SHARON, MA
CURRENT CITY: BOSTON, MA

"I once raced a man named Michael Caputo, who thought he was hot shit. We both had Centurions, and I bet him my bicycle that I could beat him across town. In the end I won, and when I asked for his bike, he just broke down and wept in front of me. Literally, he just cried like a little girl. I took mercy on him and said, 'You can have your bike back, but you can't live in Boston anymore.' Begrudgingly, he accepted, and I haven't heard from him since.

REASONS I LOVE CYCLING
"1. I am cheap, and gas is expensive.

2. My favorite geological period is the carboniferous, and it kills me to just light those poor bastards on fire. Early amphibians JUST learned to get onto land in the Devonian. Can't we show them some respect?

3. I hate gyms, but my metabolism is slowing from age."

ILYA BRUKHMAN

AGE: 18
HOMETOWN: EAST BRUNSWICK, NJ
CURRENT CITY: PROVIDENCE, RI

STEVE TORTORELLI

AGE: **24**
HOMETOWN: SAN FRANCISCO, CA

I am very lucky to be riding again!

Yulya Truskinovsky

AGE: 27
HOMETOWN: MINNEAPOLIS, MN
CURRENT CITY: BOSTON, MA

This is Yulya's winter bike. A little while
back, her summer bike, a pristine red Vitus,
got caught under the tires of a moving
truck ... along with her right leg.
"I am very lucky to be riding again!"

CURTIS ANTHONY

AGE: 51
HOMETOWN: PHILADELPHIA, PA

The shape of Curtis's mustache mimics the upturned handlebars on the old high-wheel bicycles in his shop in Philadelphia. Between his shop and his apartment on the fourth floor are two floors bursting with classic bicycle frames, parts, and ephemera. Curtis gave us the grand tour—vintage English- and French-built bicycles, wooden bicycles from the 1800s, Fred Delong's custom-built Schwinn Paramount, a Jack Taylor and Hetchins from the '60s, Curtis's Bob Jackson trike, boxes and boxes filled with Bianchi Cambio Corsa Hubs, Stronglight 57 cranksets, the first Campy derailleur. The three stories were so tightly packed with his collection that we could hardly move about, and many of his most cherished or rare bicycles were buried beneath hoards of other remarkable bikes. When Curtis repositioned them out of the way, he addressed them all directly with a "Hello, Bike" or "Hello there, friend," and in that moment we knew that we had met a true cyclist.

SEAN REILLY

HOMETOWN: WARWICK, NY
CURRENT CITY: BOSTON, MA

TONY FAST

AGE: 27
HOMETOWN: PHILADELPHIA, PA

I first met Tony riding around New York during the Bicycle Film Festival. He kept up with some of the most experienced freestyle riders in the country . . . in an almost full-leg cast.

jeremy Dunn

AGE: 29
HOMETOWN: LANCASTER, WI
CURRENT CITY: PORTLAND, OR
FOUNDER OF EMBROCATION CYCLING JOURNAL

ERIC BONNIN

AGE: 46
HOMETOWN: PARIS, FRANCE
CURRENT CITY: NEW YORK, NY

"Even just over the past few years, New York City has made so many great improvements to become more cyclist-friendly."

Carmen Wilson

AGE: 24 / HOMETOWN: SEATTLE, WA

BEN ROBERTS

AGE: **22** / HOMETOWN: GRASS VALLEY, CA
CURRENT CITY: SACRAMENTO, CA

SAM HAWKINSON

AGE: 20 / HOMETOWN: SEATTLE, WA
CURRENT CITY: PORTLAND, OR

BRENDT BARBUR

CURRENT CITY: NEW YORK, NY
FOUNDER AND DIRECTOR OF
THE BICYCLE FILM FESTIVAL

Brendt gets less sleep than anyone else
involved in cycling culture, and yet his
enthusiasm for bicycles is unparalleled.
He devotes every waking moment to
putting together a festival that not
only supports bicycle advocacy, but also
captures the heart, imagination, and
adventure of riding a bike.

Samson Hatae

AGE: 23 / HOMETOWN: LOS ANGELES, CA

Matthew Prell

AGE: **24** / HOMETOWN: LOS ANGELES, CA

JESSE SHAPIRO

HOMETOWN: NEW YORK, NY
CURRENT CITY: BOSTON, MA

BOB KAMZELSKI

HOMETOWN: PHILADELPHIA, PA
FRAME BUILDER, BILENKY CYCLE WORKS

RAMON ALATORRE

AGE: 21
HOMETOWN: SAN DIEGO, CA

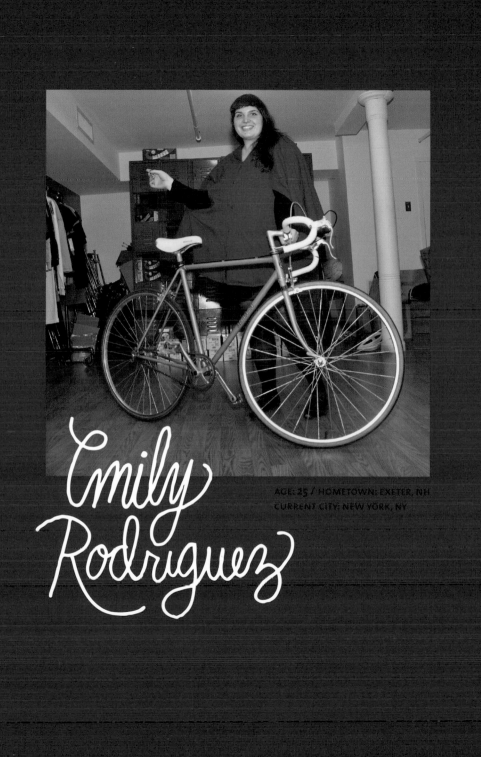

Emily
Rodriguez

AGE: 25 / HOMETOWN: EXETER, NH
CURRENT CITY: NEW YORK, NY

PETER CANNON

AGE: **42** / HOMETOWN: SEATTLE, WA

MATT MALINOWSKI
CAITLIN RUBIN

HOMETOWN: BOSTON, MA

BRANDON
EMERSON
& BOWIE

HOMETOWN: SAN DIEGO, CA
CURRENT CITY: SEATTLE, WA

NO, NO, NO!
YOU'VE GOT TO GET A SHOT OF ME RIDING MY **BIKE!**

VICTOR Matthews

HOMETOWN: NEW YORK, NY

VADIM AKIMENKO

AGE: **28** / HOMETOWN: ORLANDO, FL
CURRENT CITY: BOSTON, MA

"Basically, it's all about style." Vadim grew up down south with a penchant for loud records and classic cars—in high school he drove around in a '57 Chevy rust-bucket. "I knew that I wasn't going to have the fastest car, but I could make it look cool." It is with this sentiment that he built his bicycle, aptly named Betty White, to commute back and forth to his butcher shop in Boston.

Basically, it's all about style.

ANDREW WEYER

The best part about riding his 1990 Haro Group 1A around the city: "The babes!"

NORA LIDDELL

HOMETOWN: LOS ANGELES, CA / CURRENT CITY: NEW YORK, NY

EDWARD DEMASO

JED JENG

HOMETOWN: BOSTON, MA

CODY TERRY

AGE: **18** / HOMETOWN: SACRAMENTO, CA

NICOLA PEZOLET

HOMETOWN: QUEBEC CITY, PQ, CANADA / CURRENT CITY: BOSTON, MA

"I love riding my 3-speed Robinhood early in the morning. It wakes me up and allows me to think about the forthcoming day. I also love to hear the sounds of the city when I ride around."

jordan hufnagel

AGE: **28** / HOMETOWN: INDIANAPOLIS, IN / CURRENT CITY: PORTLAND, OR
FRAME BUILDER, HUFNAGEL CYCLES

"Sometimes it's hard to find a place to lock up because so many people ride bikes here!"

96

Clark Filio

AGE: 21 / HOMETOWN: CINCINNATI, OH
CURRENT CITY: BOSTON, MA

JESSE ALFORD

AGE: **27** / HOMETOWN: SACRAMENTO, CA

Louie Gomez

AGE: 32 / HOMETOWN: AZUSA, CA

LOUIE GAVE US THE ONCE-OVER BEFORE BREAKING INTO A SMILE.

A cyclist in Los Angeles told us that if we wanted to see some beautiful bikes, we should walk into the tattoo shop across the street and ask for Big Louie. When we entered the shop, Louie gave us the once-over before breaking into a smile and wheeling out these two award-winning, custom low-rider bikes.

Caitlin Barry

AGE: 23
HOMETOWN: BRAINTREE, MA
CURRENT CITY: BOSTON, MA

RYAN JORGENSEN

AGE: 32 / HOMETOWN: SEATTLE, WA
CURRENT CITY: PORTLAND, OR

"I had a party at my house for my birthday in late October. When all of us decided to head downtown, we did a count and it turned out that almost everybody had a bike. Those who didn't have one took one of my spare bikes or skateboards, and more than twenty of us rallied and headed down this huge hill taking up all the lanes, screaming, laughing, and shooting off fireworks as we rode. The slow-motion memory of all my friends on bikes—together, smiling, bathed in the light of roman candles—it was one of the most perfect moments of my life."

Carolyn NGo

AGE: 22
HOMETOWN: LOS ANGELES, CA
CURRENT CITY: SAN DIEGO, CA

"Riding my bike is the best way
to explore new places without
going too fast or too slow."

PATRICK THAMES

AGE: **38** / HOMETOWN: SAN DIEGO, CA
CURRENT CITY: PORTLAND, OR
BLOGGER, PEDAL CONSUMPTION

BEAVER BEAVS

AGE: 25 / **HOMETOWN: MAR VISTA, CA** / **CURRENT CITY: LOS ANGELES, CA**

"It's funny. A few of my friends used to meet up in L.A. for this ride called 'Mellow Mondays.' My friend Rob and I decided to go check it out. Well, there was nothing mellow about this Monday. We rode 15 miles to the meet-up spot, a good 70 miles on the ride, and another 15 miles home. Afterward, we all wolfed down burgers. So much for that ride!"

JUSTIN DALVE

AGE: 31 / HOMETOWN: SACRAMENTO, CA
CURRENT CITY: SAN DIEGO, CA

"At age 9, I was busting no-footers over a
15-foot double with my mom lying down in
the middle. Yeah, I was a crazy little kid!"

yeah, I was a crazy little kid!

Karen Pace

AGE: 36 / HOMETOWN: SCARSDALE, NY
CURRENT CITY: PAWTUCKET, RI

Ben Turner

AGE: **27** / HOMETOWN: DERRY, NH / CURRENT CITY: BALTIMORE, MD
CAKE ENGINEER, CHARM CITY CAKES

"Everyone started riding to work last summer, and the bikes
began to take over the bakery, so the city put in a bike rack
for us right outside!"

ERIK NOREN
BOB PARLICA

HOMETOWN: MINNEAPOLIS, MN
FRAME BUILDERS: PEACOCK GROOVE CYCLES
ERIK: "When I get passion, I build cool bikes"

McKenzie Hart

AGE: 21 / HOMETOWN: SUN VALLEY, ID / CURRENT CITY: SEATTLE, WA

JOHN CARDIEL

AGE: 36
HOMETOWN: SACRAMENTO, CA

Skateboarding legend John Cardiel woke up in the hospital one morning after an accident and could not feel his legs. Doctors told him and his family that he would never walk again. Although his life revolved around being mobile, John did not waste a single moment feeling sorry for himself, and instead began to rehabilitate his body with determination, support from family and friends, and inexhaustible positivity. From the moment he could walk again, it was all about bikes.

John Cardiel's eyes light up when he talks about bicycles. When watching him jam on his Cinelli Track Bike brakeless through the streets of Sacramento, it becomes clear that he has the ability to master any arrangement of wheels beneath him.

AGE: **24** / HOMETOWN: BUFFALO, NY / CURRENT CITY: BOSTON, MA

CORY PRIVITERA

SEAN MARTIN

AGE: 30
HOMETOWN: ANCHORAGE, AK
CURRENT CITY: LOS ANGELES, CA

"The best part about riding in Los Angeles is my
homies—the best crew anyone has ever ridden
with. We push each other to go faster every day."

MATTHEW "DEVOTION" BROWNE

AGE: 31 / HOMETOWN: LOS ANGELES, CA / CURRENT CITY: BROOKLYN, NY

"Have you not seen my ass in cycling shorts?"

Dream Bike: "The silver '62 Masi Special that my friend Michael purchased new, directly from Faliero at the Via Arona shop, below the banks of the famed Vigorelli Velodrome."

OWEN ROBBINS

HOMETOWN: SIMSBURY, CT
CURRENT CITY: BOSTON, MA

KYLLE

HOMETOWN: LOS ANGELES, CA
TRACKOSAURUS REX!

ViVi Nguyen

AGE: 19 / HOMETOWN: HUNTINGTON BEACH, CA
CURRENT CITY: SAN DIEGO, CA

SHAWN DASILVA

CHIAKI ARATA

AGE: 29 / HOMETOWN: DARTMOUTH, MA
CURRENT CITY: BOSTON, MA

"Anytime I travel, I take my bike, and I know that
I can make friends anywhere in the world."

AGE: 21 / HOMETOWN: TOKYO, JAPAN

"When I was in high school in Tokyo, my friends
and I would meet up every morning and ride to
school. It was a good 45 minutes away, so it gave
us a chance to talk and share stories. I loved that
bike—it was a really common bike in Japan
called a Mama-chari."

MIKE TOMIMITSU

AGE: **27** / HOMETOWN: GLENDALE, CA

JASON GALLACHER

AGE: 32 / HOMETOWN: BOCA RATON, FL / CURRENT CITY: BROOKLYN, NY / FRAME BUILDER, AFFINITY CYCLES

ADAM MARTINEZ

AGE: **19** / HOMETOWN: SAN DIEGO, CA

Oliver Henderson

AGE: **19** / HOMETOWN: PORTLAND, OR / CURRENT CITY: PROVIDENCE, RI

jonathan brennan

AGE: **29** / HOMETOWN: SALEM, OR
CURRENT CITY: BOSTON, MA

Armando Quiros

AGE: 34 / HOMETOWN: BOSTON, MA / FRAME BUILDER, QUIROS CYCLES

ALEXANDRA CARLSON

AGE: 22 / HOMETOWN: MIAMI, FL / CURRENT CITY: BOSTON, MA

"I love riding in Boston during the winter. I hate the cold, but it is awesome riding around the city and seeing the few cyclists brave enough to face the snow, ice, and freezing temperatures. I now know a lot of people on my route to work, and we have formed seasonal friendships as if to say, 'You're out here too, huh? Good for us!'"

FRANKIE ANGULO

AGE: 25
HOMETOWN: ORANGE, CA
CURRENT CITY: SAN DIEGO, CA

SAMUEL LUNA III

AGE: **20** / HOMETOWN: POMONA, CA
CURRENT CITY: PORTLAND, OR

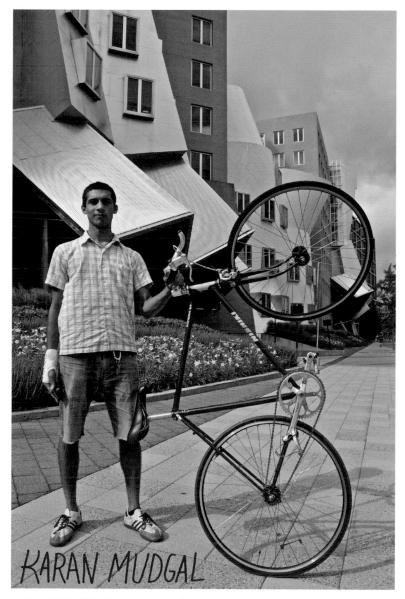

KARAN MUDGAL

HOMETOWN: LIVERPOOL, ENGLAND / CURRENT CITY: BOSTON, MA

A.M. HULCOMB

AGE: 25 / HOMETOWN: SEABROOK, TX
CURRENT CITY: SAN FRANCISCO, CA

NOAH MANION

AGE: 23 / HOMETOWN: PITTSBURGH, PA
CURRENT CITY: NEW YORK, NY

julian flores

SAM ANDERSON DANGER

ASLIHAN NIKSARLI DANGER

HOMETOWN: SEATTLE, WA
CURRENT CITY: BOSTON, MA

HOME COUNTRY: TURKEY
CURRENT CITY: BOSTON, MA

JOHN NUNN

AGE: 24
HOMETOWN: PHILADELPHIA, PA

NUNN IS #1!

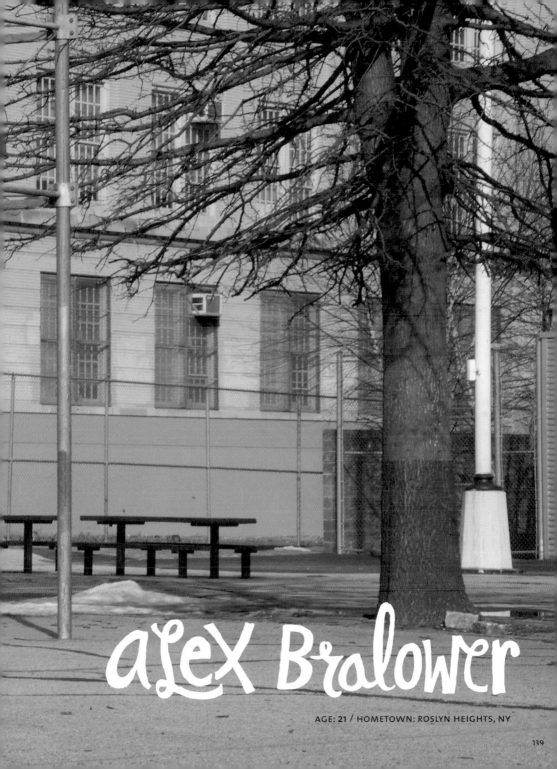

alex Bralower

AGE: **21** / HOMETOWN: ROSLYN HEIGHTS, NY

LARRY SILVA

HOMETOWN: SANTA MONICA, CA

JAMES CONNAUGHTON

AGE: 26 / HOMETOWN: WESTPORT, CT
CO-OWNER, WHEELMEN CO.

KEVIN DANIEL CONNAUGHTON

AGE: **27**
HOMETOWN: WESTPORT, CT
CO-OWNER, WHEELMEN CO.

143

VICTOR OUMA

HOMETOWN: NEW YORK, NY
A FOUNDING FATHER OF MONSTERTRACK AND
AN ORIGINATOR OF THE ALLEYCAT.

LINDSAY FROMM

AGE: 26 / HOMETOWN: MORGAN HILL, CA / CURRENT CITY: SAN FRANCISCO, CA

MARTY WALSH

AGE: 30 / HOMETOWN: BOSTON, MA
FRAME BUILDER, GEEKHOUSE BIKES

AMANDA HAGY

AGE: 27 / HOMETOWN: BIXBY, OK / CURRENT CITY: NEW YORK, NY

"Riding in New York City makes me feel so strong and capable. It's liberating in the most brilliant way, you against traffic and you against yourself. How hard can you push?"

ERIC THOMPSON

AGE: 21 / HOMETOWN: LEXINGTON, MA

"My first bicycle was a Schwinn Stingray. I used to do 180° skids in the rain when I was 7 years old. That thing ruled!"

Chris Piascik

AGE: 28 / HOMETOWN: CLINTON, CT

CLARENCE SMITH JR.

AGE: 36 / HOMETOWN: SEATTLE, WA
CURRENT CITY: BOSTON, MA

The effort that I put in in the saddle yields instant rewards.

BRANDON BOYD

AGE: **34**
HOMETOWN: LOS ANGELES, CA

Baelyn

HOMETOWN: LOS ANGELES, CA

DANIEL MUELLER

AGE: 25 / HOMETOWN: MEQUON, WI / CURRENT CITY: BOSTON, MA

JOHNNY EARLE

AGE: **28**
HOMETOWN: HULL, MA

JONATHAN BAILEY

AGE: 45
HOMETOWN: BINGHAMTON, NY
CURRENT CITY: PORTSMOUTH, NH

First Bicycle: "The first bicycle that I bought with my own money was a light blue metal flake Krystal Racer purchased from my next-door neighbor. I think I paid half and my dad paid the other half. I loved that bike, but I only had it for a month or so before I ran it, and my left knee, into the headlight of a Chevy Vega going really, really fast during my early-morning paper route."

Longest Ride: "Nine days with Mark Brooking in high school. I think we were 15. We did a big loop through the Adirondacks —I think about 1,300 miles— and it was wonderful. I want to go again!"

Best Component on Your Bike: "Basket, without a doubt. I can't believe I've spent most of my life without one."

Favorite Place to Ride: "The best ride is to the farmers market with my daughter in the WeeRide and flowers hanging out of the basket on the way home."

AGE: **28** / HOMETOWN: GLOUCESTER, MA

J.T. HARGROVE